EVOBA

The Investigations Meditations 1976-78

Steve McCaffery

The Coach House Press Toronto

All quotations from Wittgenstein's
Philosophical Investigations are based on the
English text of the third edition, translated
by G.E.M. Anscombe (New York: MacMillan
Co. 1968) and utilize its paginations
and divisions.

Canadian Cataloguing
in Publication Data

McCaffery, Steve
Evoba

Poems.

ISBN 0-88910-360-7

I. Title.

PS8575.C33E88 1987   C811'.54
C87-094935-7
PR9199.3.M22E88 1987

pro captu lectoris habent sua fata libelli
Terentius Maurus

However much men may shudder,
philosophy must tell all.
D.A.F. de Sade

Nothing so old as a new book.
Pattison

If the aim of philosophy is, as Wittgenstein claims, to show the fly the way out of the fly-bottle, then the aim of poetry is to convince the bottle that there is no fly.

The writer enters with a sign around his neck
that reads:

there is a blank space where
the faces of the audience should be
he writes in that space about
the spaces used to fill it:

under the pen is a fish-mouth
inside the mouth is a stone

in the stone runs a river entering
a porch by a pebble fence

by the fence is another way
which leads to a lake

over the lake a green parrot
is made to fly

low and close to
the level of a different lake

it is made to observe itself
but it disappears beneath the surface

of the word

water

the water in this space
disappears

a reader enters.

Logic is a mechanism
made of infinitely hard material

and logic
cannot bend

the steel wheel 'rolls' but
a wheel made of butter goes

on rolls

                    (explanation linking with
acceptance
                    not

its cause
                    (to make you walk
                    along a river when

the reason is
the road you went.

But suppose you hated me ...

then the molecules in the sofa
would attract the molecules
in your brain

there are a lot of things
i am ready to believe e.g.

that dream reported from
a height descending
from a sea of flowers
a woman sees inside a nasty way
to make things have
intolerable smells

or else the time she put
a live fly in

the head of a doll agreeing
this
     to be
           'an instance'
in the mind

but in the meantime
everything is what it is
and not another thing

and another thing
i heard you claim that

evidence of bleeding's just
a drop
       in the bucket

there isn't a difference if
you look at

           (a) what it is

           (b) the known alternatives
               to milk

meaning is the game that it appears in
a bridge a play of cards dealt else

the part we walk across
a face to make the poem
                 a 'lovely' poem

the pshit

a lovely 'shytte'.

It's an unknown land
a known behaviour in
an unknown sound

                    krasthytikkkotl
sythiololopupop

                    their actions fall
into confusion
                    confessions that

                                        I does it he
                                          does it
                                                i
                                          do
                                        I   t

without logic in a circle it's
the circus

                    'guess'
        'intend'

but this is how it strikes him
                    in the game
                    of the sentence
                    in the friction

how can he know what it is
to continue?   how would it look
                        if it
                                struck wood?
                would
algebra, intuition,

                        doubt 'what'

(one)   (thing)
                    is

an escape

a microscope

a single

sensation

just,
'guessing the thoughts' when,
            'the sky is'
                        always the hardest part

            and seeing someone writhing in pain
            from an evident cause
            in not thinking.

                        *

it is music (it's
the scraping of fiddles)
        and it fits

                        i hear a noise and call
                        it music just
                                        to make you
                            sad
                                i draw a face for you

a little closer than a larger nose

you'll say

'the face looks different
somehow it's
                because of certain
consequences'

i hear a door

shut.

        you say
they both are sad
i say
        it has exactly

this expression.

                *

Shuffle:

        214
            1. 2. 3. four.

            2. two. too. to. 2wo

                            with this

            there is
                    a *thing.*

shape
intention
too
    also   the rule
        or the rule but *blindly*

it's how it would look if
'hole' was 'patch'

'this is how it strikes me' + 'the whole patched up
was all that remained'
                re:
                    meaning.

wrong

the black word in its
white surround

'guessing clouds' & concluding
that nothing's as difficult
as sky

how it would look
when inclined to say
blue

'a kind of ornamental coping that supports

nothing'

any choice traces the lines in space
there's rails but not rules
and time
doesn't fit.

(a section of the rail laid
invisibly
to infinity

or the sentence i don't choose
to speak me

rules

that refer to refuse

```
as my eyes travel   ...................................  D
as my eyes obey    ...................................  H
as my eyes listen   ...................................  T
as my eyes see     ...................................  K
```

```
           H
        D
           T          one word
        K
```

interwoven
and see you.

          day,
                                segment of
                 that way?
                                addition of
expansion!

            two ex plus one squared tomorrow
            and
                 'see you'
                          goes to make up
            say how . . . . .
                             feeling of
                             being at
            the fact of agreement

'tech'
     'nique'
             a matter of course

. . . . . paraphrase of
. . . . . expansions of

                      ex/pression

situation ....
surrounding ....
.... identity

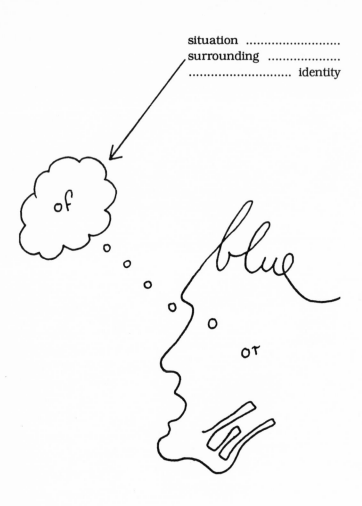

a rule
a word or
a blank
        left for it

                tracing its line through
                the whole of space:

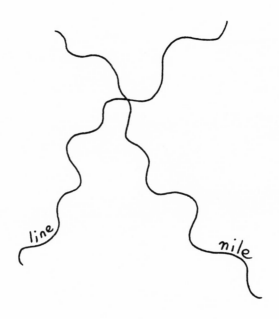

line

nile

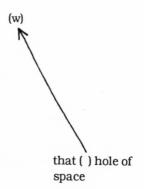

(w)

that ( ) hole of
space

You are reading when you *derive*
the reproduction from the original.

P.I. 65e 162

             red colour
blue   red definition   sky
             red judgement

                          a private syntax &
                          a common language

'has'

                          'something'

             once you know what
             you know, once
             it was a whole use
             he had

                          to the right
                          of a meaning out of sequence

memory:
             in time
             in page
             in process

                                a dictionary (inwardly)
                                a table

then her lips
her eyes
             the pain of a wheel

or what each thing would like to say

in short her pain meant her symptom guessing
how the clock might serve her

time
        in different things
                            'comment'

        'exemplar'

presuppositions of the left hand's size
imagined by the right

        red pain(t) and fitting in
        the word

                I casts
        to say itself.

in this privacy
        of place
        of pain
does she know
what she has?

or how her meaning moves
to mean
        to not refer?

the red she has means the red not
what the red is
she refers to
        or the red as 'the' red
she uses and the red 'she'
doesn't use

'I turn to stone but my pain goes on'

you hurt your hand
so it writes the word

        pain

        right +
        wrong &
        ————

        not at all.

he puts his hand on her head to prove
how tall she is
                    (almost
he doesn't prove a thing

it's all a trick
in a state of mind

call the room

'i am asked to go away'

'i say at the end'

'i left when i learned it'

'discovered'[4]

'judgement'[3]

'motive for a movie'[7]

these are shut.

sixty years old
it was a room
this is the broom but

brush

an answer to anyone

correct.

Once upon a time a blank wall
permitted a sequence of doors
in a room.

       familiar sentence language

familiar
experience

l
      t
  e

      t

          s

e
    r

           f a m l i a r
           . . . . . .
           . . . . . .
           . . . . . .
           p o s s i b l
           . . . . . .
           . . . . . .
           . . . . . .
           m o v me n t

he   (moves)   to 'go' (to go to) 'whistle

        someone
        intention

        reply

                'that i am right'
'what i have left'
          correction/direction to

(what) 'i' what (do) 'what' not (where)
   'he has whistled'

          the   in.

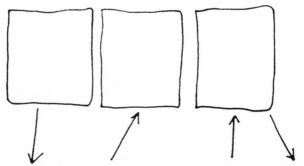

(pictures on the wall's intention to describe as it were
how the facts fit
what the walls do hang)

'this'

and between:

how a thing looks how
that thing looks at you
the word 'beetle' in a box
the way place takes
possession
how if everyone said it . . . . . .

surrounding surrendering

the self
the box
(the thing
)
the is

sensation

pictured steam or syntax
washing or saying a pot shows
no information

imagine this   γ

      that   b i   d

          pressence moves (shows)

      that
your words.

             (thyme)

hour silences.

As long as
capacity is

as single as
a sentence sentence as

different as
what is word

reducing
(us-in) what/is

        lacking to us
        'somehow'

               (where)

   (there)

                   (   )
      (are)
  (none)
   (

         (of)
)
            (us)

  (

)
     (she combs her hair)

(and sees it)
    (first familiar)
        (then unfamiliar in
        the light)

(in the room)   (she remembers a table)

    (of age and)   (time)
  (read off from any)

       (clock)

conviction

      in as much as 'click'
      gets said

her memory the picture
in a past that shows all rooms
                as 'A'

      (B) in the room
      compares
           the object with
           its picture:

there's sky by the window and
a will to say
      blue

         with a *genuine* voice.

His body on the balance in the grammar
she no longer knows

is the signal

                        producing words 'i can go on'
          say 'see'
                    as a guide into any part

he can walk to her
touch her
or again the sentence

'he couldn't understand'

                              'walking'[8]

          'thinking'[5]

                    'deciding'[2]

an altitude laid flat inclined to say
. . . undertone
               dimension of depth
what the same words might mean in
other shapes.

cf. perhaps:

your hair the last
that is but
first think of it

as being

there is a lake a like
the ob-ist as-if it reaches you
liking
in this (similitude)
to likening

a fact
a face
a smile

to home

of thoughts
of albums
of photographs

sketches of
remarks of

stimul   i
stimul   us

Such as s.u.c.h.

        the paradox, the passion
        the inhibition &
        the panic

        an inner process taking place
        so:
            what difference could be greater?

to imagine
     the *private*
          exhibition

looks/as
     if we had denied them
     to deny him.

'The expression of the body cannot lie'
saying 'say' with
your mouth to your throat
it tells a truth
in these words ...

'which are his dreams
           of   s u ture
                   tr c
                  s u ture

as he walks his hands
are the things he sings of
a day or a neck
a syllable seed
the wind calls 'blue' beneath what it does

the sky and the size
and the window:

                        pane

        gains

                curtains

                          rains on
what is neck that intersects is
doing
      to dying things
what 'he snores'
                as a this
for a that never
here
      as a there:

he leans on a stick that isn't explained
makes time
                what he imagines
drawing flesh in a cube
as well
          a solution

at the square where
he stands
he defines the word
                  'sepia'

the length of the syllables 'as pie'
in Paris squares
of colour as if
             to exist

                          . . . when in Rome

. . . do as
           . . . alone

done in that language.

Sometimes

        'this'

           and other objects

a forest as simple as
(bits of wood)
          knot named
the 'bare' name innocent
as 'somebody' somewhere someone's
sketch
      of the face
from a meaning a mind a movement a verb

his thought becoming pressure
under a weight of stone

'flat speech' when it is

and what it is
to be

a pause
in.

verb
plus a body

then it flames
'to build a fire'

she builds a fire
without saying it

she misses it.
we merely miss.

she knows hair as she knows fish.

The agreement, the harmony, the thought
and the reality
end the reality

he says
            this isn't red and pointing
to the words that make the tongue
puts
      a ruler to his lips

'to measure'
                  'inch'

there is a foot of speech
'in' 'this'

or a lump of wood
or a stupid block to even say
this is the gulf between

the order &
the execution

—————————————————————————

every line by *itself* seems dead

dead as he is
now

alive
in this use

justification quite literally comes
to an end when we say 'play'
and the grammar of the word called language
connects with the grammar of
the world re-named 'invent'

He says:
            come on ... the sentence changes
            to become
                        his walk

RIGHT

LEFT

it's a question of
the proper doorways

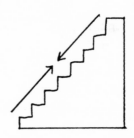

UP

DOWN

the mechanism oɪ response
is to a certain kind of influence

the arbitrary necessity
of stairs

he doesn't climb
but learns by claiming.

Can there be a collision between picture and application?

P.I. 56e 141

cl 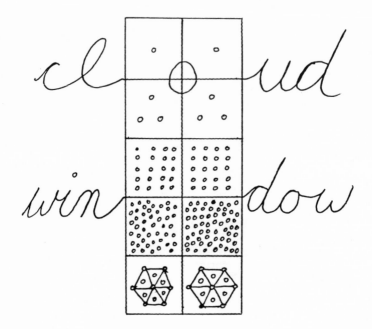 ud

win dow

May i say 'brown'? This

shows a chart in
a multi-coloured square

a description of patches
the mental pains in a day

I am here
in a common space / face:
a (visual) reality behind
the chin's particular temptation
to think this is a chain
of occult peculiar
connexions
            I in the eye of
'i have pains'
                denotative
        possibilities of blood

red as a wound or
he read it in Tolstoy

a green parrot trisecting
tunes in music
                the vowel (which is
'why'
        the world is yellow'

Calculus:
            the pseudo-statement in a picture puzzle
            to philosophize odd-jobs
            to prove
                    a proper name improper in

a mould
a mouth
a muscle

its acid reacts in a copper cage
a parrot whispers to a certain tune
the gramophone experienced
as rules of chess through smoke

feeling the rails they came on
the simple accident of being trains

elaborate pastness
                    inclined to say
that this i call
the tune
        inflexes gesture
the red and the green
as the patches of incident.

In a dim lit room
you merely see the writing
a sign
a parrot sings
a sentence that enters

see the colour you say
turn your head in a peculiar direction
it is the eye that places you
before you point out faces

Place:
        is an order
        a direction where
        the metaphor is atmosphere
        and you are under
                  this particular assault

there is a day
a boundary line
a sentence called senseless
a muscle sensation
in the ordinary experience
of seeing a hand.

the word is charged
with my desire

can the word (not) negate?

trees are not rope
and string

is knot tied

it is there
but being here

it never can be
here

it
is

as such
not as it will

(not) be

what

is
is

not
the question
that is

what is
as is   is   ais

          o   as   is

Language is a labyrinth of paths. You approach from one side and know your way about; you approach the same place from another side and no longer know your way about.

P.I. 82e 203

I see a world i am not present to
a cinema
the eyes
       a walk prevented

'where:
       i cannot go to when'
                 i see it

the screen becomes the barrier
the scream goes through
the place
       where light is gathered

scattered.

'an assemblage'

'a cutting room'

there is a door
when S appears as G

or else
a case of scotch

as in a case of murder
through drink

and just in case and if a scream does occur (it is her)
it is a chain between these persons (it is him)

S to the side of an old wall sees
G appear inside a doorway offering drinks to friends

eyes (he said 'e' she said 'yes')
with ears appears to be teas and occurs

to posit voices in position
desire is speaking its own word and desire

is simply the only chance
to take off your pants and wipe your mind

he burns the library in the cause
of a slight panic in the head

the brain in the head &
the shoes on the mind &

so efficiently
                    he slices 'off' the nose
to alter
his own concept of

the passport.

You have pains or
you should have

          in the mouth
          with her hand
          with his finger

the clear terminus
of 'suppose'

two double basses playing out
an appendectomy
          as a sort of pattern
          in the mind
            the mind in-sorts

the plain fact would be this:
the child has burnt itself
          it's in the past
          & felt the pain

a locus in
a distance

there's no fear if the pencil
pierces the hand
          which writes of 'ground'
'particulars'
          'assumptions'

think of a greeting
and thank you

and note a parrot frightened by fire
and see a photograph in words.

The words he learns have taught themselves
these facts:

what I writes is
what i does not speak

although others are present
in a way

in its manner of speaking

a word spoken
an open door

before that
'it's a disclosure doing
the talking

getting things seen
in one another'

a door i.
e. what the word is about when it's shutting up

in speech
it slams

(he's listening by speaking
what it says to him

twenty nine pages apart

the image by an image making
a flow of words a hill in speech with
something like language
over the top of
we   (genetic)   (primacy)
            and   say

I thinks of the room its in
& there's nothing interior about it

outside the words
a man sits speaking silent to all
but himself

but i'm looking at you
in the process of looking in the process
by which

you decide what i am

and language lies there
a slice of meat i'm cutting into
slices slicing in
the rules

so you say speech is
a chewing of the meat i'm cutting rules into
so that i actually chew this meat as words

it's all happening on the basis
of this become in that.

59

AAAAAAAAaaaaaaaAAAaaaaaAAAAAaaaggggGGGggHHHHhhh

A a   g G H h

  a   g   h

HE HAD NOT YET DISCOVERED THE PRESENCE OF
DIFFERENTIAL ELEMENTS BEHIND THE PHONEME.   *blue*

AT ANOTHER LEVEL
HIS POSITION INDIRECTLY PREFIGURES *green*
THAT OF THE OTHER   *pink*
WHO WAS CONVINCED THAT STRUCTURE
IS OF THE ORDER OF   *yellow*
EMPIRICAL OBSERVATION
WHEREAS STRUCTURE
IS IN FACT

BEYOND IT.   *black*

The house is devouring the mirror
his silk tie

the same night a loose lash entered
his eye via

the veins of
the choroid

minute particulars
in themselves
                    the head
                    the mind

opaque or mechanistic
whatever she draws

takes time
among the curtains obtestations

in the southern noise
from pipes appears

a dress ring
on her little finger

to the right of
what appears correct

these fingers are integers
that objects move

from the dress ring
on the little one

'finger'
that is

the wedding ring
becomes

a third inside the house
the mirror wants

61

she takes time along this formula
in every integer

complete a unit
still impossible to move

her hand
that same night entered

his eye.

And necessary
in this passage ring to ring

the second finger obtestates
the first

the finger (integer) inside
as yet unborn anterior to all

that moves
from dress to ring

the mirror in the mirror
where the weddings are

three rings appear
the wedding ring finger

not addressed
the dress (ring) (finger) raised

to put
(wedding) in

the place of (dress)
yes

as yet unborn
a consequence the place of

(placed-as 'as' placed-in)
the wedding that appears

the ring the second integer alone
the mirror of the mirror of

the other ring:
the three.

Since everything lies open to view there is
nothing to explain.

P.I. 50e 126

Beyond the door
to your door

           is my door his
           & theirs

on the stairs
but above the entrance

          (possibly)

the word is clouds
with beyond it
           clouds beyond

the order of
empirical observation.

Everything is already
there

in the dead line direction
is a surface

when we mean a page
we move

(going up to the thing we mean
it misses us)

forming the current when
con/tent with form

a form of order shows

but an order orders
its own execution

the door
in the room in

language

      exit:
          draw a circle around the mental process
          of an expectation

          call it a head and sail
          a thought on it until

a gun
begins

a shout
a sh
a sho   t

and the red you see is
not the red
      expected

          so i dreamed last night of the word pain
          in my arm lodged
          by the tongue as a bullet would

... and the noise filled my arm.

It is pain it is red and
it is in it

so what does he see to say
to see
        there are patches regions

a surface to things
on stones named 'plants
                    in our skin'

terms in
        his larynx
        her larynx

(the same brain goes for the same 'in' his brain

said.

this.

     what?

i have learned from these.

A sentence on the hand
a picture obtruding

on the other hand
he can't enter his house

as a visual room without
owner

so when i do 'this'
i am said for example

          to speak in a new way of
          her grammatical chair is

          a new kind of
          song.

   sense.

      complete.

        &.

          perhaps.

he points once
to a tree

he points again.
there is

a forest.

Interiority

Give him no directions
whatsoever.

Don't tell him what
he *actually* is.

Now watch his imagining
this situation.

It's a crowded street and there's everyone in pain.
They conceal the pain and so
it didn't describe their bodies.

They leave their pain take
paint on themselves and leave
their bodies behind.

If i imagine this
look at the world 'think'
'it *must* be different

to laugh to be
imagining
when i imagine.'

This way
someone does a sum
in his head

there is a bridge
an oscillation outside
of a machine

at which there is no
pretending
to arrive.

These are the signs to someone else.
I is not my
just as here is not there

my i's grown tired and
there's no one here to groan
to know

a book is a foot
a foot is a body
in sensation without names

anaesthetized and parallel.
this is a sign to
someone here

the sky and drinking
by light & your brain
by its processes

are ears which are
deaf to a self
they hear they are

blind too
in the unbridgeable gulf
called

the this.

they stand on their toes
to invert their meanings

has a word as

a body moves.

To puzzle the walk
you go by it.

Nothing is written
of the frame

it's pencils
draw the line you step across

the category:
'numbers'

                         '–' slab

    ' – – –' patterns

        '– – –' colours

                'Go to Hell'

at the fifth bolt
he stops

she imagines a series
of different cases

                        'to ask about the facts
                            she feels?'

no demand at all.

I's who i am &
here's where i is & 'this'
is not a name

... the dawning of an aspect
        in a picture of a face until
        she smiles

a mirror to that usage.

an order
a picture
a poem
a sentence

      something new in plain view

a system
a theme in music

two kinds of wheel

          a spell.
          a sphere.
          a star.

a table,
a taste,
a tautology,

          a telegram;
          a tendency;
          a tension;

        the microscope:
        some milk   :
        a mistake   :

if i say, but
if he says

we might be

alluding

this. and. this. and. this.

the colours deny it's
a move in chess

in this case
he gets stuck at

purple has difference.

'If we had no memory we should be at the mercy
of a sample.'

P.I. 28e 56

The dream he dreams
'if a lion could talk'

i see him see you shut your eyes
they seem to say he seems to see
if i say

      look

(he's looking over there
                here)

is a tree behind his eyes
where they make a mistake

                      (that goes for me too!

when i say it say

look

      (it's a fashion we see when
        the whole is
               filmed.

'i never learnt i was a point on the point of pointing'

to likenesses
to limits
to lions

to a map
to a law
to a drop.

You colour me
red or
you colour me 'circle'

she colours me blue
they colour me twice

a read slip in a language
two lips spelt
tulips, these
are the important facts.

In a state of
UN

i
pretends to be conscious

i am only a machine.

a parrot
a gramophone

_____

a healthy relationship?

so the parrot says:
'i'm actually dreaming'

and the gramophone echoing
'He ought to know'

the parrot pretends to be
a false assertion

the gramophone talks
in its sleep

eventually
they engage in phantasy

it is blue and a space it is
conscious it is playing

      it is raining

they go to sleep with the usual feeling
they lift that weight and the talk of thinking

a cloud drifts by
a bubble which manifests a frame

in their arms

to lift a weight
to take a place

voluntary
   in
voluntary

The gramophone dreamt when it told the dream
of a human shape

called 'pain'

        set: a drift in a neck

a connexion

        we only call pain what has
        this position

so it can't be
here.

The wound is a calculation
in the head
about the foot which kicked a stone

under the surface
how far have you got?

        (smiling

      one wants to say

          circumstances)

she says that a scientist
has
    no soul

a parrot reports this as a fact
that sometimes grammarphones react.

She smiles her name in normal play
and classifies the sheep
by what they shape

'but a ship is not a shop'

in his theory the parrot is wrong
it has drowned in speech
far from being heard

the rule of the parrot is the determinate degree
of its elasticity

walls don't move

all things are rigid
where the surface looks like this

beneath the parrot it says
'satisfied'

      (pictures
           under the illusion they're
      presenting essences
             late
consumed in advance

in a sense)

well
  ell
  ell
  ell
  ell
  ell
  ell
  ell
  ell

Psittacan digits plus

a code:
(clause):

derivations from the parrot's
mechanical foreseen
unreliable form   (claws):

in the mind a pattern
even feathers misfire.

In some shadows
a solution

strongly traces lines.

Look at this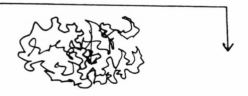

(your way of seeing there was
a parrot in a room)

(dimensions,
shapes,
etc.

the particular lighting in a square
there *is* no house
& it *was* a gramophone
see the colour you say:

cloud

(& also)

'because of this'

de-severance.

It pays to be counting parrots

   'also'

       'haphazard'

the fact of a man.

I point to paper a parrot names
red
    imagining

i saw a pencil move
a glowing coal inside
a stage of paint

(perhaps he meant   parallelipiped)

 perhaps it rains

(*that's settled*)   'that's'

an iron nail which scratches the glass
saying
     'can't'

(. . . apples with labels
    in different hands   he stands

    by a gramophone)
               in a brain
               in a box

    inner pain

The moon (is) rises.
The family (when) plays.

This locomotive is a concept
the parrot just

happens to guess a headache's
not a hexagon

imponderable strikings
which fade

take it or leave it
it still doesn't rain

problems
        (attached to
                -ed saying 'I can'
                -ed following a rule
                    that I do

either you learn the language
or learn the learning of what language is

a green parrot in perspective
but the rest of my body
inconceivable

something (strange) is happening
when example

        'this is a pencil'
        'this is a wood'
        'this is hard'
        'this is round'

& the parrot eats it all

        hypothesis:

    a locality

       next:

  second

       multiplication: oui

'An infinitely long row of trees is simply one that does *not* come to an end.'

P.I.   110e   344

Sentence beginning
the left hand . . . . .

in the visual field
the parrot smiles

dictionary definition
behind the left eye . . . . .

sentence beginning . . . . .

(there are no complications)

it leads to what is
different:

      a tissue

      a sneeze

the flight of a bird
the explosion of the word mine

the sneeze (ends) the flight (ends)
the explosion (ends)

the bird
        (. . . continues . . . we were
trying to escape when this appeared)

as knees
as the flight of a bird

a tissue in a mine . . .

        (this (ends) the knees this (ends)
         the flight this (ends) the tissue

the bird: 'which'

            continues . . . we were
        trying to escape this when that appeared

that sneeze
that flight of this bird
that tissue in this mine

                this that (ends) the sneeze
                this that (ends) the flight
                this that (ends) the tissue

94

                                    There is a quantity
                                    of two falls equivalent to

                                    valentines & statements
                                    that a cat might choose
                                    to paw

appear appears
appearing &

apart from this

snow fallen (twice)

it must be this:

                                    that there's a quantity
                                    of two to

                                    falls of snow
                                    as red assed
                                    as truth can be

snow standing
still

apart from that the light
resembles these marks
you know & you
suppose

                        some are particular

'there is a house'
'there in a tree'

classes
individuals or just

                        ontologies

the apparatus mapped 'behind'
the curtain where
it seems unlikely that there is
a parrot mapped apart from the word
that put it there.

Long ago there was resemblance
long ago this was a fact.

It's always thursday
in her logic

the reddish reason showing
pinker on

a scaffolding of facts
he falls from into

                    r   r
        r
                r   r
        r   r
    f i c t i o n
                            r
                r
                    r
                        r
            r   r
            r

in his eyes is still
the place of pain

her gladness feeling
sadness is a somewhere

after all
they are not

words 'and after'

a sensation of secretion

the descent of a permanent cloud.

In the actual use of expressions we make detours, we go by sideroads. We see the straight highway before us, but of course we cannot use it, because it is permanently closed.

P.I. 127e 426

The book exploded in his hand.
Slowly, at first

And so, too, a corpse seems to us quite inaccessible to pain.

P.I. 98e 284

dead

Editor for the Press: Christopher Dewdney
Cover design: Gordon Robertson
Author photo: Rory Maclean
Typesetting: Nelson Adams
Printed in Canada

For a list of other books
write for our catalogue
or call us at (416) 979-2217

The Coach House Press
401 (rear) Huron Street
Toronto, Canada M5S 2G5